¡Puedo ser lo que quiera! / I Can Be Anything!

PUEDO SER BIBLIOTECARIA
I CAN BE A LIBRARIAN

Anthony Ardely
Traducido por / Translated by Eida de la Vega

Please visit our website, www.garethstevens.com. For a free color catalog of all our high-quality books, call toll free 1-800-542-2595 or fax 1-877-542-2596.

Cataloging-in-Publication Data

Names: Ardely, Anthony.
Title: I can be a librarian = Puedo ser bibliotecaria / Anthony Ardely.
Description: New York : Gareth Stevens Publishing, 2019. | Series: I can be anything! = ¡Puedo ser lo que quiera! | Includes index.
Identifiers: LCCN ISBN 9781538227367 (library bound)
Subjects: LCSH: Librarians–Juvenile literature. | Libraries–Juvenile literature.
Classification: LCC Z682.A73 2019 | DDC 020.92–dc23

First Edition

Published in 2019 by
Gareth Stevens Publishing
111 East 14th Street, Suite 349
New York, NY 10003

Copyright © 2019 Gareth Stevens Publishing

Translator: Eida de la Vega
Editorial Director, Spanish: Nathalie Beullens-Maoui
Editor, English: Kate Mikoley
Designer: Laura Bowen

Photo credits: Cover, p. 1 (kid) nataliya/Shutterstock.com; cover, p.1 (background) Andersen Ross/Blend Images/Getty Images; pp. 5, 13, 23, 24 wavebreakmedia/Shutterstock.com; pp. 7, 17 Tyler Olson/Shutterstock.com; pp. 9, 11 asiseeit/E+/Getty Images; pp. 15, 24 hxdbzxy/Shutterstock.com; p. 19 Education Images/Universal Images Group/Getty Images; p. 21 IMAGEMORE Co, Ltd./Getty Images.

All rights reserved. No part of this book may be reproduced in any form without permission in writing from the publisher, except by a reviewer.

Printed in the United States of America

CPSIA compliance information: Batch #CS18GS: For further information contact Gareth Stevens, New York, New York at 1-800-542-2595.

Contenido

¿Qué es un bibliotecario?. 4

¡Hola, señora Poe!. 8

Préstamo de libros 16

¡Vamos a ser bibliotecarios! 22

Palabras que debes aprender 24

Índice 24

Contents

What's a Librarian? 4

Hello, Ms. Poe! 8

Borrowing Books 16

Let's Be Librarians! 22

Words to Know. 24

Index. 24

A los bibliotecarios
les encanta leer.
¡A mí también!

Librarians love to read!
I do, too!

Los bibliotecarios trabajan con libros.

Librarians work
with books.

La señora Poe
es bibliotecaria.
Ella ayuda a mi clase.

Ms. Poe is a librarian.
She helps my class.

Nos ayuda a encontrar libros que nos gustan.

She helps us find books we like.

Los encontramos
en el estante.

We find them
on the shelf.

Los encontramos
en la computadora.

We find them on
the computer.

Te puedes llevar
los libros a casa.
Los bibliotecarios
los sacan para tí.

You can take
books home.
Librarians check them out.

Debes devolverlos.
A esto se le llama préstamo.

You need to
bring them back.
This is called borrowing.

Yo pedí este en préstamo.
¡Es sobre arañas!

I borrow this one.
It's about spiders!

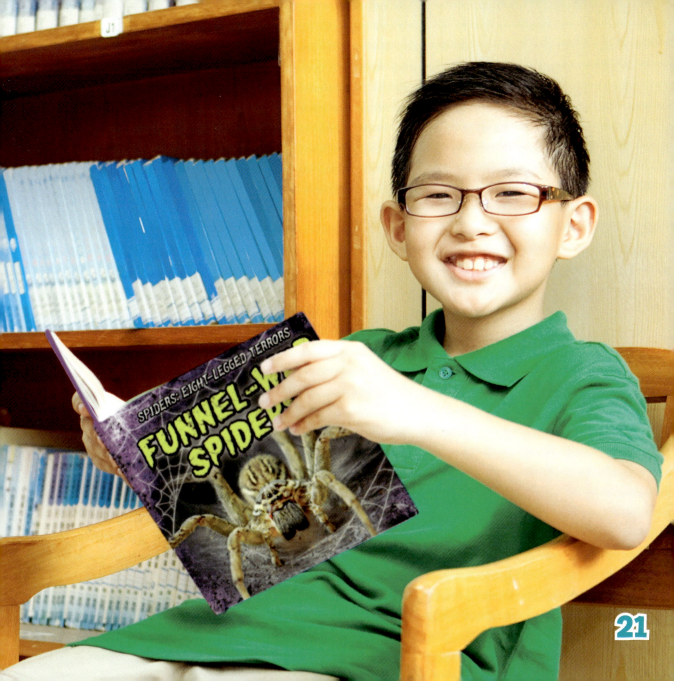

Puedo ser bibliotecaria.
¡Y tú también!

- -

I can be a librarian.
So can you!

Palabras que debes aprender
Words to Know

(la) computadora
computer

(el) estante
shelf

Índice/Index

computadora / computer 14

libros / books 6, 10

préstamo / borrowing 18, 20